DATE			

BAKER & TAYLOR

LIFE SCIENCE PROJECTS
for Kids

A PROJECT GUIDE TO
REPTILES & BIRDS

Colleen D. Kessler

Mitchell Lane

P.O. Box 196
Hockessin, Delaware 19707
Visit us on the web: www.mitchelllane.com
Comments? email us: mitchelllane@mitchelllane.com

Mitchell Lane
PUBLISHERS

LIFE
SCIENCE
PROJECTS
for kids

A Project Guide to:
Exploring Earth's Biomes • Fish and Amphibians •
Mammals • Projects in Genetics • **Reptiles and Birds** •
Sponges, Worms, and Mollusks

Library of Congress
Cataloging-in-Publication Data

Kessler, Colleen.
 A project guide to reptiles and birds /
Colleen D. Kessler.
    p. cm. — (Life science projects for kids)
 Includes bibliographical references and
index.
 ISBN 978-1-58415-874-5 (library bound)
 1. Reptiles—Juvenile literature. 2. Birds—
Juvenile literature. 3. Science projects—
Juvenile literature. I. Title.
 QL644.2.K47 2011
 597.9078—dc22
                                                    2010009241

Printing   1   2   3   4   5   6   7   8   9

                                                    PLB

CONTENTS

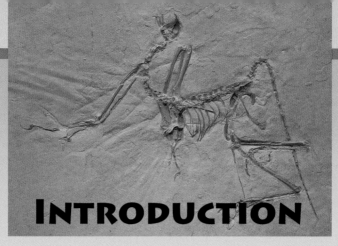

INTRODUCTION

In 1861, workers in a limestone quarry in Germany found an unusual fossil. It resembled a bird, was about the size of a crow, but had teeth. When scientists studied this and other similar fossils, they realized that it was, indeed, a prehistoric bird. The fossil clearly showed feather impressions, a defining characteristic of all birds. This find confirmed that birds had been present on Earth for at least 145 million years, and that they were related in some way to prehistoric reptiles.

Archaeopteryx, as the bird is now known, means "ancient wing." Unlike modern birds, it had claws on each wing, a flat sternum, belly ribs, and a long, bony tail. Like modern birds, its bones were light and hollow, and it had a wishbone and reduced fingers. It probably was not a very good flier. In fact, it seems to have had characteristics of both modern birds and modern reptiles. It had teeth and certain bone structures found in modern reptiles, and it lacked a horny bill.

Many scientists believe that this species was the evolutionary transition between reptilian dinosaurs and modern birds. Others disagree. They believe that birds evolved from a small group of dinosaurs called theropods, though they still debate how these dinosaurs began to fly. Did they start at the tops of trees, glide down, and eventually adapt to flight? Or did they leap high into the trees in search of food, eventually taking flight?

However they evolved, modern reptiles and birds share some similarities. Each has scales. While a bird's scales are found on its legs, a reptile's scales cover its body. Both reptiles and birds lay shelled eggs. A bird's egg is much harder than a reptile's egg, though. Bird eggs are covered in a hard calcium carbonate shell, while reptile eggs are soft and leathery.

Birds are most recognized by their feathers. This is a trait that no other modern animal can claim. If it has feathers, it is a bird. Most birds use their feathers to fly. The central shaft of a feather is hollow, keeping it lightweight. In fact, a bird's whole body has adapted to perform flight, including some of its organs.

Flight has fascinated scientists for thousands of years. Watching birds fly is what prompted humans to invent airplanes and other means of mechanical flight. Still, nothing can fly as well as a bird. Different species, depending on their size and habitat, fly in different ways. The albatross extends its eleven-foot wingspan and glides on air currents. The tiny hummingbird beats its wings up to 200 times per minute, seeming to hover as it licks nectar from plants or feeders.

While we typically think of winged creatures flying through the air when we think of birds, there are a few that don't fly. They still have feathers, but they don't use them for flight. Penguins are one example. These Arctic birds look clumsy as they waddle around on land, but they are sleek swimmers as soon as they jump into the water. Ostriches are another example. They live on land and are fast runners. Another large flightless bird, the giant moa, became extinct because it didn't have the ostrich's speed. The moa lived on the islands of New Zealand. It lost the ability to fly because there were no predators to threaten it. When Europeans came in the nineteenth century, they brought cats and rats with them. These mammals hunted the moa eggs and young, and the settlers hunted the giant adults, which were easy targets.

Most birds rely on their sense of sight to find food, avoid predators, and find safe nesting places. This is evident by the size of their eyes. Some birds, like the starling, have eyes that make up almost 20 percent of their head weight. Most birds have their eyes on the sides of their heads. This positioning allows them to see danger from almost any angle. Owls have eyes that face forward. Their eyes are large to bring in as much light as possible, assisting them in finding their prey at night. The position of their eyes gives them great depth perception for accurate hunting. As they rely primarily on their eyesight, very few birds have a sense of smell.

Instead of great eyesight, most reptiles have a keen sense of smell. Chemical receptors are located in the nose and on the roof of the mouth. Some reptiles, such as snakes, rely on their sense of smell almost exclusively. They do not use their other senses to locate prey. Some snakes, including pit vipers, have heat-sensing organs that help them locate prey as well. Most of the heat-sensing snakes are nocturnal. Their infrared sensors allow them to locate and accurately strike their warm-blooded prey in the dark.

All reptiles share certain defining characteristics. They have scales. They lay eggs, though some seem to give live birth. Garter snakes and other species that seem to bear live young actually incubate their eggs within their body. They hatch inside the mother and emerge. Once a reptile baby hatches, whether it has hatched within or outside of its mother, it is on its own for survival. Most reptile mothers do not take care of their young, though alligators and crocodiles are exceptions. Baby alligators and crocodiles stay with their mothers for up to two years, and some of these reptile moms are very nurturing. Reptiles are ectothermic. This means that their body temperature rises and falls with the temperature of the environment. Each reptile species has a unique temperature range in which it can live.

Despite these likenesses, reptiles are a diverse group. The smallest is a tiny dwarf gecko found in the Caribbean islands. It measures just 0.63 inch long. The largest reptile is the common saltwater crocodile. Most are about 17 feet long, but some can get as long as 23 feet and weigh up to 3,000 pounds.

Dwarf Yellow-headed Gecko

Birds and reptiles have interested nature lovers and scientists alike. They can be found just about anywhere, and they come in a wide range of sizes, shapes, and forms. In this book, you will learn about these classes of animals, along with some of their habits, preferences, and defining characteristics, through hands-on activities. Some of the activities are for backyard use; others can be adapted or used for science fairs and school projects. You can have fun with them all as you learn about the animals around you. Remember to respect the animals you are studying—whether you are out in their natural habitats or they are pets in yours. Be kind and gentle, and treat them carefully.

One of the greatest tools for life scientists—young and old—is a nature journal. A journal should be used with each of the activities in this book. It will serve as your record of observations and conclusions you discover as you learn about birds and reptiles. In it, you can devise your own nature investigations and record your own observations about the natural world. When you're outside with your journal, take a pouch of supplies, such as pencils, an eraser, watercolor pencils, and a small pencil sharpener.

Nature journals come in many forms. They can be binders, spiral notebooks, homemade books of paper stapled together, or leather-bound. Whatever form your journal takes, it can become an impressive record of your wildlife observations. You can customize it however you wish. Some people prefer to write observations. Some enjoy drawing or painting in their journals. Others like to combine these. In my nature journal, I write my observations, sometimes in completely flowing sentences, and other times in short lists. Sometimes I sketch what I see in pencil, sometimes I add color to my drawings. No matter how you use your nature journal, I hope you make it uniquely yours.

As with any science activity, observing and experimenting with nature requires you to take some safety precautions. Be smart and use common sense. If an activity recommends that you work with an adult, please do so. Think about what you are doing at all times and remember that there are hidden dangers everywhere. Bird feathers and nests may carry mites or germs. Eggs and reptiles carry salmonella and other bacteria. Don't breathe in chemicals, dust, or debris from the materials you use in this book, and remember to wash your hands often. If you are outside and handwashing is inconvenient, keep a bottle of hand sanitizer in your pocket or supply pouch. Sanitizers do not replace proper handwashing, but they are good to have when soap and water are not accessible.

"BLIND-LY" COMPARING WILDLIFE

The best place to learn about birds and reptiles is outside. After all, that is where birds and reptiles are found! Scientists spend time in the field observing wildlife. They need a way to watch the animals interacting with their environments, but not be seen themselves. One skill that experienced wildlife observers have is blending in. An easy way to do this is to sit still behind a blind. A blind is a hiding place that blends in with its surroundings.

While blending in and staying still sounds boring, it is one of the best ways to see animals do what they do. It is also a wonderful way to get pictures, because the animals won't be startled again and again by your presence. Birds are the easiest type of wildlife to watch using a blind. If you place yourself in a location that has a large reptile population, such as near a pond or in a forest, you may be lucky enough to observe turtles and lizards, too.

The directions that follow explain how to create a tepee-shaped blind. You can get creative, though. You could build a lasting blind out of wood and cover the walls with brush if you plan to observe from the same spot at different times. If you are in a wooded area, just find a natural blind in the form of a thick shrub or bush. Add a sturdy chair, and you are all set!

Materials
- Several long branches or saplings
- Rope (Size and length can vary according to what you have on hand. One with a diameter of $3/16$ inch or larger works well, and you might want to make sure you have several feet.)
- Leaves and brush
- Spray adhesive (optional)
- Camera (optional)
- Field guide to birds and reptiles

Procedure

1. Decide on a good place to set up your blind. Ideally, you want to choose a place where you can observe both birds and reptiles.
2. Gather your branches or saplings.
3. Tie one end tightly with the rope.
4. Check to make sure the tied end is secure, and stand the cluster of branches up, with the tied ends at the top.
5. Spread the bottom out in a circle, leaving a small space to serve as an entryway.
6. If your branches or saplings are leafy, this may provide you with all the coverage you need to observe without being seen. If not, tuck leaves and brush between the branches to add to the coverage. Use spray adhesive to help secure the leaves, if necessary.
7. Crawl inside your blind and get yourself set up to observe quietly. Have your nature journal and supplies with you, as well as a camera if you plan to photograph the wildlife that you see.
8. Look toward a location that wildlife visits, such as a pond, stream, or feeder. Draw or photograph what you see, keeping very quiet.
9. Compare your drawings, notes, or photos with those in a field guide. Try to identify what you saw.

KEEP A PHOTOJOURNAL

A photojournal is a collection of photos that document your life, your studies, or an event. It can be a wonderful tool for reliving your encounters with nature. In this activity, you will make a photojournal of a nature hike. If you have a nature journal already, set aside a few pages for your photos. Tape or glue them into place once you print them. It is important to include dates, times, and observations about your photos in your journal.

When hiking, you must be accompanied by **an adult**.

Materials
- **An adult**
- Sketchbook or nature journal
- Sticky note or small note card
- Pen or marker
- Digital camera

Procedure

1. With **an adult,** go for a walk in the woods, desert, fields, or somewhere else nearby that is known to have an abundance of birds and reptiles.
2. Using a camera, take pictures of any birds or reptiles you see.
3. On a sticky note or card, jot a quick note about each photo you take, noting any special circumstances surrounding the picture. For example, "Photo 12—a sparrow picking up twigs." These notes will help you identify your photos later.
4. When you get back home, download and print your pictures. Tape or glue them into your sketchbook or journal. Be sure to also note the location, date, and time of your observations.
5. Underneath your photos, write detailed captions. Use your notes to guide your thoughts and remind you about what you saw on your walk. Your captions can be simple descriptions of the photos, or more reflective paragraphs about what you saw and felt as you took the pictures.

BIRD CALL SURVEY

Birdsong is crucial to birds' survival. It tells others what species it is. It announces whether it is male or female. It scares intruders away from a nest. Birds can sing different songs, just as a musical instrument can produce different notes. Each one tells a different story. Birds don't have a larynx like us. They have a bony structure called a syrinx for making sounds. They use special muscles that vibrate the syrinx to make different songs and calls.

Learning to observe wild birds is part seeing and part hearing. Many species look similar, and some hide out of sight altogether. If you are serious about learning more about the winged creatures that hang out near you, it is important to identify their songs. There are many CDs and websites that teach listeners about the different sounds birds make. They share examples of these calls so that you can learn to identify the birds in your area.

Materials
- Recorder equipped with microphone (A digital recorder would be a great tool for this activity. You can record, and then upload the sounds to your computer and save them in the .mp3 format.)
- Thin rope or string
- Bird field guide
- Nature journal
- Pen or pencil
- Watch or timer

Procedure
1. Find a quiet place that is heavily populated with birds.
2. Using rope or string, secure your recorder to a pole or tree, preferably near an active nest.
3. Turn the recorder on.
4. Locate an out-of-the-way spot nearby, and sit down with your nature journal. You may want to sit in the blind you built in activity one.
5. Close your eyes, be still, and listen for several minutes.
6. Record the sounds you hear in your journal. Try to replicate the sounds you hear as closely as possible. (For example, a chickadee makes a *chick-a-dee-dee-dee* sound.)
7. Spend as long as you can quietly listening and recording the sounds you hear.
8. When you have finished, use your bird book, recordings, written observations, and the Internet if necessary to identify the birds you heard.
9. Write the species names in your journal near the written interpretations of the sounds you heard, and then make a complete list of all the birds you heard during your observation period.

POPPED OR UN-POPPED?

Many people hang bird feeders or scatter seed in their yard to attract birds. Birds eat seeds like sunflower and corn. People enjoy sunflower seeds roasted and corn popped, though. Most people don't like them raw. Do you think birds would like their corn popped like people eat it? In this activity, you will test un-popped and popped corn to see which way birds prefer their seeds.

Materials
- Two plastic dishes or tubs
- Popped popcorn
- Un-popped popcorn

Procedure

1. Find a place in your yard where you can place the dishes. It should be a place that is safe from predators such as cats, yet easily observed from an unopened window.
2. Fill one dish with popped popcorn.
3. Fill the other dish with un-popped popcorn.
4. Go inside and watch the dishes. Do any birds come to check out the offering? Which popcorn do they prefer? Do the birds like the corn the way it is found in nature? Or do they like it after it has been cooked by humans?

(**Note:** If no birds are coming to try the popcorn, sprinkle some birdseed nearby to encourage visitors.)

NEST BUILDING

Depending on species, birds may build their nests on clifftops, high in trees, or in ditches along roads. Some shorebirds build nests of rocks. Others build intricate woven cups of grasses, twigs, and down. In this activity you will try to build a bird nest. As you shape your materials into a nest that could hold a few bird eggs, think about the task. How do birds make it seem so easy?

Materials
- Twigs
- Leaves
- Dried grass or plants
- Paper scraps
- Yarn
- String
- Other fibrous materials

Procedure
1. With **adult** permission or accompaniment, walk around the neighborhood, take a hike in the woods, or search the Internet to find bird nests of various shapes and sizes.
2. Observe them carefully and try to discover how the nests have been constructed. If you are looking at real nests, try not to disturb any bird families.
3. Gather a variety of materials from the list above, and any additional nest-building materials you think would be useful.
4. Using just your fingers—no glue or tape—try to build a nest that mimics one of the nests you observed. Make sure your nest would be able to hold two or three eggs.

NESTING HABITS

Birds are amazing engineers. Some species create intricately woven homes out of hard materials such as twigs and bark. They make their homes among branches that twist and turn in heavy winds. These homes come in all shapes and sizes. From the tiny Ping-Pong-ball sized nest of a hummingbird to the ten-foot wide nests of bald eagles, birds can build incredible structures. See if you can discover how they do it by carefully dissecting a nest in this activity.

Materials
- Binoculars
- Gloves (preferably disposable latex gloves)
- Paper bag
- Old newspapers
- Tweezers
- Magnifying glass
- Nature journal
- Pen or pencil
- Field guide to birds

Procedure
1. In the late fall or early winter, go outside with binoculars and search for an abandoned bird nest.
2. Wearing gloves, gently take the nest from the tree after you've made sure that it is no longer occupied. If the nest is high up, ask **an adult** to help you get it.

3. Set up a workspace at home, preferably in the garage or on a deck or patio, where there is room for you to spread out. Line your workspace with newspaper. If you are not able to set up outside, make sure you cover your indoor workspace completely and sanitize the entire area once you have finished.

4. Use tweezers to separate the pieces of material that make up the nest.

5. Examine the pieces closely with a magnifying glass, and separate the materials into like piles.

6. In your nature journal, make a list of the nesting materials and analyze how the nest was constructed. Was there a pattern to the materials used? Did the materials give you any clues as to when the nest was built or where the bird flew to gather supplies?

7. Using a field guide or website, try to identify the type of bird that made the nest. While the best way to identify what type of bird built a nest is by observing the birds in it, or by looking at the eggs, it may be possible to draw a conclusion by looking carefully at a nest's characteristics and comparing them to characteristics listed in your guide. Look in the resources section in the back of this book for website and book suggestions.

WARNING: Bird nests may contain mites and harmful bacteria. Wear gloves to do this experiment. Dispose of the nest and gloves in an outside trash can when you are finished, and wash your hands thoroughly.

DOES COLOR MAKE A DIFFERENCE?

Like most animals, humans have eyes with two types of cells. These are called rods and cones. Rods help us see light. Cones help us see color. Bird eyes have a similar structure to human eyes. Humans and birds have more rods than cones. This enables us to see well during the day in all sorts of color. Birds, however, do not have any blood vessels in their eyes. This helps prevent shadows and the scattering of light as it enters the eye. Therefore, birds can see things more clearly than humans. Images enter without being diffused, and birds' eyes are able to get to work processing light and colors.

Humans have three types of cones, each able to see a specific color. When the cones combine, we see all the colors in our world. Birds have four types of cones. Some even have five! This means that birds can see red, green, and blue like we do, but they can also see one or two additional colors. They can also see ultraviolet light, which is invisible to humans.

With their special color-detection ability, it would be interesting to see if one color is more appealing to birds than another. Try this experiment to see if birds prefer one color to another.

Materials

- Four small wooden or wire bird feeders, unpainted
- Paint in 3 colors: red, blue, and green
- Large bag of birdseed or suet
- Scale
- Nature journal
- Pen or pencil

Procedure

1. Find a place in your yard to hang the birdfeeders clustered near each other, taking precautions against squirrels. (Hang them on poles or trees with squirrel cones or some other type of deterrent.)
2. Fill them with seed, and leave them for a one- to two-week period so birds recognize the feeders as a food source and begin to frequent the location.
3. Following the introductory feeding period, take the feeders down and paint three of the feeders each a different color. Leave the fourth unpainted.
4. Do you think color will matter to the birds? If so, which color do you think will be most attractive? Write your hypothesis in your journal.
5. Fill each feeder to the top with seed and weigh each, recording the weight in your journal. Date all entries in your journal.
6. Put feeders out for 48 hours.
7. Bring feeders back in and weigh them. Record the weight and refill each.
8. Weigh the feeders again and record the new "full weights."
9. Replace the feeders outside and leave them for another 48 hours.
10. Repeat the procedures every two days for two weeks.
11. After two weeks, subtract each end weight from the start weight and average the amount of birdseed eaten from each feeder over a two-day period.
12. Revisit your hypothesis. Did color matter? Which color feeder was most attractive to the birds that visited your yard? Why do you think you saw these results? Is there something you could do differently the next time you performed this experiment?

SO SWEET

Hummingbirds are fascinating little creatures. They are tiny birds with a very high metabolism. This means that they must feed constantly because they continually use up their energy. In fact, a hummingbird needs to eat about every 10 to15 minutes! Hummingbirds are diurnal. At night, a hummingbird's body goes into torpor, a state of rest, so that it can recharge before flying off the next day in search of food.

Hummingbirds are found only in North and South America. They can live from southern Alaska to the tip of Chile. The majority of hummingbird species are found in the tropical habitats of South America. In fact, more than half of all hummingbird species are found there! The ruby-throated and black-chinned hummingbirds are the most common types in North America.

A hummingbird's diet consists of small insects and nectar from various flowering plants. Although hummingbirds have a long beak, they actually lap up nectar with their tongue. Making a solution of sugar and water is a common way to attract hummingbirds to a backyard garden. In this activity, you will see if hummingbirds prefer one type of sugar to another.

It is important to note that nectar is only a part of a hummingbird's diet. It's the quick energy that gives them the fuel they need to track down the important stuff—insects and spiders. Insects and spiders give hummingbirds the protein, vitamins, and minerals they need to be healthy. So hummingbirds use nectar from flowers and sugar water from feeders to keep their energy up as they hunt for the more nutrition-packed food they need.

Materials
- Different types of sugar (available at most specialty grocery stores, health food stores, or online):

  Sucrose—Common table sugar, sucrose comes from sugarcane and sugar beets and is very sweet.

  Fructose—Found in fruits and vegetables, fructose is more than 1½ times sweeter than sucrose.

  Maltose—Maltose comes from heating and adding water to malted barley. This sugar is not commonly found in nature, and is usually manufactured.

  Glucose—One of the main products of photosynthesis, glucose provides energy to an animal's brain. It comes naturally from corn, maize, rice, and wheat, and is half as sweet as fructose.

  Mannose—A sweet secretion from birch and beech trees, mannose can also be found in cranberries, blueberries, corn, and white potatoes. It is half as sweet as glucose.

- Small lidded jars to store the sugar solutions
- Small plastic syringes (the type available for medicine dispensation in drugstores) with milliliter markings
- Marker
- String
- Nature journal

Procedure
1. Make a sugar solution for each of the sugars you are testing. Each solution should be three parts water to one part sugar. Store the solutions in labeled jars.
2. Fill syringes with 10 mL of solution, one type of solution for each syringe. Label each syringe with the type of solution it holds.
3. Using the string, hang the syringes in the yard or over a deck or patio near places that hummingbirds frequent.
4. After 24 hours, measure the amount of liquid that has been consumed from each syringe. Which did they prefer?

BIRDS OF A FEATHER

Feathers are crucial to a bird's survival. They serve as identification within species. They provide insulation, keeping birds warm. They also allow most birds to fly. They have a hollow shaft in the center that gives structure without adding weight. Each shaft has a vane made up of many barbs projecting from it. These barbs have barbules (little barbs) that cling. As you observe feathers in this activity, note how these seemingly simple objects are amazing examples of nature's wonder.

Craft store feathers are safer to use in this activity than wild feathers. They are still from real birds, but are collected and sanitized carefully. They are safe to handle, yet still show the unique characteristics bird feathers share. If you decide to use feathers you find outside, be sure to wear gloves.

Materials
- Craft store feather
- Gloves
- Scissors
- Magnifying glass
- Microscope
- Tape measure
- Tape
- Piece of notebook paper

Procedure

1. Using a magnifying glass, examine your feather from top to bottom. Record observations in your nature journal.
2. Carefully cut through the center shaft of the feather. What do you notice? How does what you observe help the bird fly? Record your observations.
3. Do you see that the central shaft of the feather is cylindrical? A cylinder is one of nature's strongest shapes. This gives the feather strength while keeping it hollow so it stays light.
4. To explore the strength of nature's cylinder, take your paper, hold it upright, and try to balance one of your materials on it. It doesn't work, does it? The paper won't stay upright and immediately bends when you put any weight on it.
5. Now try rolling the paper into a tight cylinder and securing it with tape. Try balancing the same object on the paper now. Does it hold? It should.
6. Try pressing down on your tube. It takes some pressure to make it crumble. The cylindrical shape of the bird feather's shaft creates a natural power source.
7. Now, look carefully through your magnifying glass at the surface of the feather. What do you notice about the vane? Record your observations.
8. Using the microscope, look more closely at the barbs that make up the vane of the feather.
9. Brush backward against the barbs to separate them. Look at them through your magnifying glass. How might this disturbance affect flight?
10. While looking through the magnifying glass, smooth the barbs back into place. Do you see the tiny hooks (barbules) catching each other to keep the feather in this smooth state? Record your thoughts and observations.

While the feather may be light and strong, it still needs to be able to push against the air to keep the bird in flight. When the feather is smoothed, the barbs create a solid wall to push back against air, creating resistance. When the barbs are disturbed, tiny holes open that air could go through, reducing the resistance needed to fly.

POLLUTED WATERS

As you discovered in the previous activity, bird feathers are lightweight, strong, and wind resistant. What happens, though, when human actions prevent feathers from doing their job?

Water pollution can hurt the environment, including the plant and animal species that live there. Most water pollution comes in the form of oil or other harmful chemicals that have been dumped or spilled into lakes, streams, rivers, and oceans. The pollutants travel through the water source, affecting plants and animals near and far.

When oil gets on a bird's feathers, they cannot do the job that nature intended them to do. Oil enters the structure of the feathers, opening them up. This keeps them from sitting close to a bird's body to insulate it and keep it warm. Oil also weighs birds down, making it difficult for them to float properly on the water. Birds whose feathers are coated in oil cannot fly well, and they may have difficulty finding food or escaping predators. Oil can be swallowed by birds too. Birds take very good care of their feathers. They preen often. This means that they clean themselves and fluff up their feathers. When oil-covered birds clean their feathers, they swallow pollutants, become sick, and eventually die.

Materials
- Craft store feathers
- Gloves
- Magnifying glass
- Microscope
- Paper towels
- Water
- Oil—motor oil works best for this, but cooking oil can be used as well (Note: If using motor oil, please have **an adult** help you.)
- Pipettes
- Dish detergent

Procedure

1. As you did in the previous activity, take a feather and look at it under the microscope. This time, focus on just the barbs. Study the way they overlap. This overlap provides waterproofing for the birds' bodies. Water rolls right off.
2. Dip your feather into a cup of water. Pull it out and examine it carefully. What does the water do? Does it soak in? Bead up? Drip off?
3. Dry the feather by gently pulling the feather through a folded paper towel. Did it dry? How quickly? When birds get wet in nature, they can easily dry themselves by shaking off the water and smoothing their feathers out.
4. Using a pipette, place a few drops of oil in the water.
5. Put on gloves. Dip the same feather in the oil and water. Again, look at the feather carefully. What happened to the feather? What does the oil do on the feather's surface?
6. Dry the feather with a paper towel like you did before. Does the oil come off? What happens? In the wild, birds are not able to get the oil off their feathers, either.
7. Now try to find out the best way to clean an oil-slicked feather. Dip two more feathers in the oil and water so that you have three soiled feathers. a) Try washing one in cold water. b) Wash another in hot water. c) Wash the third in hot, soapy water.

Washing with water alone isn't enough to remove the oil from a bird's feathers. Hot soapy water works best. Wild birds that have been affected by oil pollution become weak and sick very quickly. They are not able to regulate their body temperature well. They need to be kept at a healthy and constant temperature. Therefore, volunteers who help clean up oil and other pollutants in water use warm water and work quickly to help birds survive.

EGGSHELL CHEMISTRY

Bird eggs have a hard calcium carbonate shell. Amazingly, this hard shell forms on its own as it passes through the oviduct right before it is laid. The oviduct is the passageway that leads from the ovaries, where the egg forms, to the outside. On the membrane that surrounds the yolk and albumen inside the egg, there are points where columns of calcite form. These columns continue to form side by side until a shell encloses the egg. (Calcite is a form of calcium carbonate and the necessary ingredient for forming hard eggs.) The shell hardens when it reaches the air as it leaves the bird's body.

Reptiles do not secrete calcite. They lay soft, rubbery eggs. In this activity, you will remove the calcium carbonate from an eggshell. This will allow you to see what a bird's egg is like just before it leaves the bird's body, and what a reptile egg is like.

Materials
- Two eggs (from the grocery store)
- Two jars with lids
- White vinegar
- Water
- Paper towels
- Nature journal
- Pen or pencil
- Vinyl tape measure
- Slotted spoon

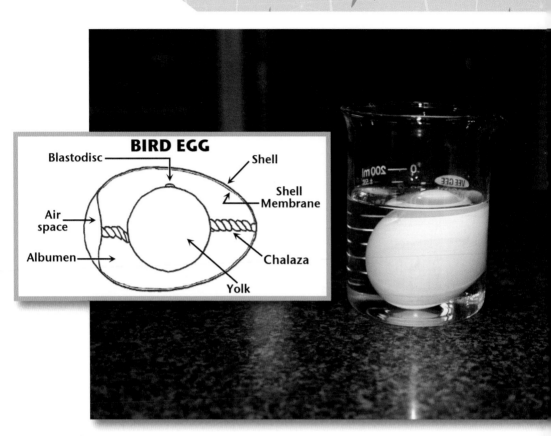

BIRD EGG

Blastodisc
Shell
Shell Membrane
Air space
Albumen
Chalaza
Yolk

Procedure

1. Observe the eggs before placing them in the jars. Draw what they look like, record their measurements, and write a description of their color and texture.
2. Place eggs in separate jars.
3. Cover one egg with water and put the lid on the jar.
4. Cover the other egg with pure vinegar and put the lid on the jar.
5. Every six hours, check the eggs by taking them out of their jars, drying them with paper towels, and recording measurements and observations again.
6. After three days, use a slotted spoon to carefully remove the eggs from the jars.
7. What do you notice about the shells?

The vinegar is an acid that removes calcium carbonate. The shell that has been soaking in vinegar will resemble the rubbery eggs of many reptiles.

WHAT EGGS-ACTLY IS THE DIFFERENCE?

Reptiles and birds both lay eggs. While bird eggs have hard outer shells, reptiles have soft, leathery shells. Some, such as the eggs of lizards and snakes, are very soft. Other reptile eggs, such as those laid by turtles, are harder, but all are softer than bird eggs. There are differences inside, too. Compare the two types of eggs in this activity.

Materials
- Gloves
- Chicken egg
- Diagram of a reptile egg (on page 29)
- Pointed scissors
- Small dish
- Magnifying glass
- Nature journal
- Soap

Procedure
1. Wearing gloves, open a chicken egg by tapping the shell with the point of a pair of scissors. Continue tapping until you are able to break a small hole in the shell.
2. Insert the point of the scissors and gently cut an opening.
3. Remove the loose pieces of shell.
4. Enlarge the opening if it is smaller than the yolk.

SNAKE/LIZARD EGG

Blastodisc

Shell (rubbery)

Yolk

Shell Membrane

Albumen

5. Carefully, pour the contents into a small dish.
6. Examine the shell with a magnifying glass.
7. Do you see the pores? Record your observations.
8. Locate the shell membrane and air space. Record your observations.
9. Examine the yolk. Can you find the blastodisc? How about the chalazae? Record your observations.
10. Inspect the albumen. Record your observations.
11. Compare the diagram you made of the chicken egg with the diagram of a reptile egg. What are the similarities? The differences?

When you are finished with the experiment, dispose of the eggs and wash the dishes with soap and hot water. Throw the gloves away and wash your hands thoroughly.

SNAKES IN THE GRASS

One common type of reptile is the snake. Snakes are predators. Depending on the species, they will eat eggs, small mammals, birds, frogs, and sometimes other reptiles. Snakes can locate their prey through smell, vision, or even thermosensitivity. This means that they can recognize the heat coming from another animal's body and follow it.

Snakes rely on camouflage to protect themselves from predators, such as hawks and eagles. Many snakes are poisonous: they can bite and impair a predator to defend themselves. Their coloring, though, provides the best defense. A snake's scales resemble the coloring of its habitat. In this game, you will see how coloring helps snakes blend in with their surroundings.

Materials

- Colored craft sticks—these can be purchased from a craft store, usually in packages of 150-200
- A yard or, if you don't have a yard, a park with grass
- Partner
- Blindfold
- Timer
- Other types of ground, such as sand, soil, and asphalt (such as on an empty parking lot)

Procedure

1. Sort the craft sticks by color.
2. Choose 10-15 of each color, then mix them back up.
4. Go outside and blindfold your partner.
5. Scatter the sticks across a patch of grass.
6. Set a timer for five minutes, and untie the blindfold.
7. Have your partner collect as many of the scattered craft sticks as he or she can before the timer goes off.
8. Take the sticks back inside and re-sort them, recording the number of each color found.
9. Did your partner find them all? Which color was the hardest to find?
10. Do the experiment again, but this time have your partner throw the sticks into the grass, and you try to find as many as you can in five minutes.
11. Did you find them all? Which color was the hardest to find? Were you and your partner able to find the same number of each color?
12. Keep playing the game, but scatter the sticks across other types of ground, such as sand, soil, or an empty parking lot.
13. Compare the success rate for you and your partner for finding each color on different types of ground. How does this information help you understand a snake's need for defense measures like camouflage?
14. If you did not find all the sticks during the game, go back outside and look for the rest. You do not want to leave craft sticks all over the ground.

SLITHERY SNAKES

There are several main ways that snakes use their bodies to move. Most snakes use one or two of these methods for most of their movement, but they can apply any of them if a situation requires it. The type of movement used depends on the type of surface, the snake's body size and shape, and the temperature of the ground and the air.

The most common type of movement is lateral undulation, or serpentine. Waves of muscle contractions move down the snake's body toward its tail. As the snake makes contact with bumps on the ground or a rough surface, it pushes off those objects and moves forward.

Concertina locomotion requires a snake to pull its whole body into tight bends, then straightening itself out. It is named after the concertina musical instrument—which is like a small accordion—because the bends in the snake resemble the bends of that instrument.

Sidewinding is perhaps the most recognizable motion. Sidewinders send a wave of movement down their body. This rolls from head to tail and lifts sections of the snake's body into the air. It brings its tail forward, then lowers its body. The snake moves diagonally forward when compared to the direction the head and neck are facing. A similar motion is called slide-pushing.

Rectilinear motion is a slow, straight movement that happens when large snakes use their belly scales to grip the ground and creep forward.

Snakes can also climb, jump, and coil up and strike. They can even use a corkscrew motion, similar to lateral undulation, to swim.

The key to a snake's ability to move, though, is friction. Snakes push off from whatever surface they are moving on, and their scales grip it using friction. They have special muscles that allow them to move scales individually or as a group to get a strong hold on the ground. In this activity, you'll explore how friction may help snakes grip different surfaces. Then, you'll observe either a real snake or an online video to see snake locomotion in action.

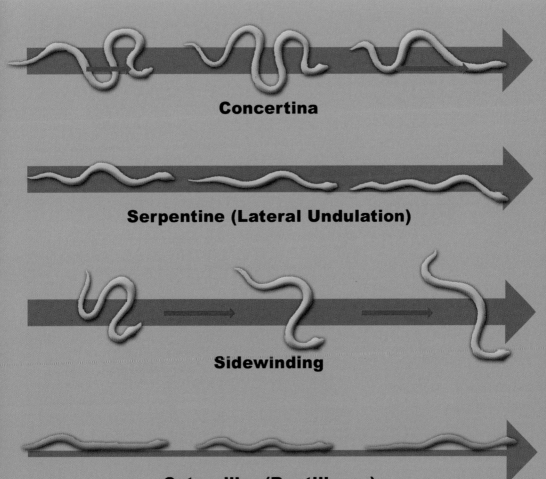

Concertina

Serpentine (Lateral Undulation)

Sidewinding

Caterpillar (Rectilinear)

Materials

- A piece of string or yarn, about 2 feet long
- Flat object such as a small book
- Tape
- Sheet of plastic wrap approximately 8" by 11"
- Sheet of aluminum foil approximately 8" by 11"
- Sheet of notebook paper approximately 8" by 11"
- Sheet of rubber approximately 8" by 11" (available at hardware stores)
- Pet snake or online video of snake locomotion (such as "The Secret of a Snake's Slither" by the National Science Foundation)

Procedure

1. Tie a piece of yarn around a book by placing the middle of the yarn between the pages and pulling it around the spine.
2. Tape a sheet of plastic wrap to a flat surface such as a tabletop.
3. Place the book on the plastic wrap and pull it across its surface using the excess string. How difficult was it to pull?
4. Repeat this activity by pulling the book over each material: foil, paper, and rubber. Think about how difficult it was to pull the book across each surface. Record your observations in your notebook.
5. Which surface was the most difficult to move the book across? This surface provided the most resistance for your book. This resistance is friction. Snakes use their scales to create resistance, or friction, to move across the ground.
6. If possible, observe a real snake move. Perhaps you have a friend with a pet snake or you can visit the zoo, a pet store, or a nature center. If observing a real snake is not possible, then check out some of the many videos online. A link to the National Science Foundation's video mentioned above is included in the resource section at the end of this book. You can also do an Internet search for snake locomotion and find numerous videos and websites with photographs. Be sure to get **an adult's** permission and to click on only safe sites. The best websites are those maintained by universities, science foundations, and departments of natural resources. You will know these sites by their web addresses. They end in .edu, .gov, and .org.

MOVE LIKE A CROCODILE, GROOVE LIKE AN ALLIGATOR

Perhaps the most feared of all reptiles are crocodiles and alligators. These mighty beasts have powerful jaws that clamp down with more than 70 sharp, pointed teeth. Their bodies boast a thick, armored hide. They slink and swim, hiding in marshes and swamps and along riverbeds. Because their eyes are on the top of their head, they can be almost completely submerged and swim up behind prey before they are even detected. They are opportunistic predators, which means that while their diet consists of mostly fish, turtles, and small mammals, they will eat whatever they can catch—even a human!

Have you ever seen a crocodile or an alligator move on land? They move in three different ways. The belly crawl is the walk that people think of when they picture crocodilian movement. Their body seems to move side to side in a staggering motion. This type of movement is usually used for short distances. The high walk is when a crocodile pushes itself to a tall stand. Its belly is off the ground and its head is high. It can see far ahead like this, so it uses this type of walking to move greater distances. The most unusual method a crocodile uses to move is the rare gallop. The strangest characteristic of the gallop is that the legs don't move the way they normally do. Usually they move in an alternating way— left front, right back, right front, left back, etc. When galloping, the back legs push off at the same time, propelling the animal forward. The front legs catch the ground, and the back legs gather for another push.

Materials
♦ Wide, open space
♦ A couple of friends to try this with you

Procedure
1. With your friends, lie facedown on the ground.
2. Bend your arms.
3. Extend one arm and push off with your opposite leg, alternating to move yourself across the ground. This is the belly crawl.
4. Now push yourself up so that your belly is off the ground. Walk the same way you did while belly crawling. This is a crocodile's high walk.
5. Before you try to gallop, roll over onto your back. Try walking like a crocodile now. Is it possible? Why or why not? What do you think a wild crocodile would do if it found itself on its back? A crocodile must use its tail to flip itself back onto its belly in order to walk.
6. Now try galloping. Move your back legs at the same time, pushing off the ground. Then push with both hands at the same time.
7. Try finding an online video of crocodile movement (try "The Crocodile Is Fast"). Search for crocodile or alligator locomotion. Or, search for specific types of walks like the belly crawl. Compare an actual crocodile walking to your simulation. How did you do? How did your friends do?

SNAKE SNIFFERS

Snakes rely on their sense of smell to help them find food, get away from predators, and locate a mate. But they don't smell with a nose like we do. They smell using their tongues! A snake shoots its tongue in and out, up and down. Inside a snake's mouth are two openings. These openings lead to a sensitive organ called the Jacobson's organ. Snakes touch their tongue to this organ and rub off the scents that they have gathered. Then, the Jacobson's organ sends a signal to the brain, which tells the snake what has made the scent—food, predator, or mate. Can you imagine having to rely on your sense of smell to find food and friends? See what it would be like in this activity.

Materials
- Index cards
- Cotton balls
- Blindfold
- Timer
- Scented oils and extracts—such as peppermint, almond, vanilla, lemon, or lavender
- 8 or more people to play the game

Procedure

1. Using separate cotton balls, swab each scent onto separate index cards. On a final card, swab the same scent as one of the other cards.

2. Blindfold one player and hand him or her the card that has the scent that matches another card. This is the snake.

3. Give each of the other players an index card and have them spread out, holding their cards up in front of them.

4. Turn on the timer and have the snake walk around and try to find its mate (the player with the matching scent).

5. Once the snake finds its mate, check the timer.

6. Mix the cards back up, choose a new snake, and see if he or she can beat the first snake's time.

7. Think about it: What is it like to rely on your sense of smell like a snake does?

COLORFUL CHAMELEONS

Different reptile species have unique characteristics. One of the most interesting of these may be the "magic" of the chameleon. A chameleon is a tropical lizard that can change color from green to red, yellow, brown, or even blue! These changes can happen in as quickly as a few seconds. The chameleon's outer layer of skin is transparent. There are special pigment cells called chromatophores in three separate layers beneath this transparent layer. The first layer contains xanthophores, which are red and yellow pigments. The second layer contains guanophores, the blue pigments. The third layer contains the darkest pigments, black melanophores. The chameleon's brain sends signals telling the chromatophores to mix, and different pigments blend together to form a wide range of colors.

Scientists believe that chameleons change color for many reasons. They believe they change color based on mood or temperature, and to communicate. They don't, however, believe that chameleons change to blend in with their surroundings. They think that certain colors convey different messages to other chameleons.

How can chameleons take on so many varied colors with only red, yellow, blue, and black to work with? This activity will help you find out.

Materials

- Newspapers
- Five small jars or bowls (baby food jars work well)
- Water
- Ink or dye in the following colors: red, yellow, blue, and black
- Pipette or straw for each color
- Several test tubes (available at science supply stores) or more baby food jars
- Test tube rack or an extra jar to hold tubes

Procedure

1. Cover your work surface with newspapers.
2. Fill each small jar or bowl halfway with water.
3. Pour dye into jars, coloring the water so that you have a jar of red water, yellow water, blue water, and black water. Leave one jar half full of clear water.
4. Using a pipette or straw, remove a small amount of water from a jar and put it in a test tube. To do this with the straw, dip it into water, then put your finger over the top before drawing it up from the water. Do not take your finger off until the straw is over the test tube.
5. Add water from a different jar of colored water. What is the new color?
6. Experiment by trying to darken and lighten the color using black and clear water.
7. How many different colors were you able to make? How many variations of each could you make using the black and the clear water?
8. Challenge yourself to make as many colors as there are in a box of crayons. Is it possible to achieve all of those colors with just red, yellow, blue, and black?

ENDANGERED CHELONIANS

Turtles, tortoises, and terrapins all belong to the scientific order Chelonia. Scientists call them chelonians. They are all reptiles, have scales, and are ectothermic. So why do they have different names? Their names come from where and how they live. If you know the name of a species, you will understand some of its characteristics instantly.

A tortoise is terrestrial—it lives on land. Tortoises are found in warm climates. Their feet are like clubs with short toes. Most of them have high, dome-shaped shells. When a tortoise pulls its head into its shell, it is able to completely seal its shell to protect itself from predators. Giant tortoises can reach over four feet in length, weigh up to 500 pounds, and live for more than 150 years.

Turtles are either completely or mostly aquatic—they live all or most of their lives in the water. They have webbed feet that make it possible for them to swim well. Sea turtles are able to swim especially well. Their feet are flippers. Sea turtles live completely in the water, only coming out to lay their eggs in the sand. Freshwater turtles swim well, and catch their food in the water, but they also climb onto rocks and logs to bask in the sun. Take a walk near a pond one sunny day and you might see these chelonians stretching out and soaking up rays!

Terrapins always live near water but spend their time divided between land and water. Terrapins are usually small, and they are commonly sold as pets. They tend to be found in the dark, brackish water of muddy ponds and swamps. Like any reptiles, terrapins, turtles, and tortoises can carry salmonella, so it is important to wash your hands thoroughly after handling any of them.

Many chelonians are endangered. In this activity, you will use Internet search engines and websites to find out why these reptiles are threatened.

Materials
- Computer with Internet access
- Paper and art supplies

Procedure

1. Using a computer with Internet access, learn about turtles, tortoises, and terrapins and why they are endangered. Some websites to start with are included below. (All web sites were current at the time this book was published. It is important to have **an adult** check these links with you before you begin.)
   a) World Wildlife Foundation: Marine Turtles
      http://www.tinyurl.com/yajfr7u
   b) Caribbean Conservation and Sea Turtle Survival League
      http://www.cccturtle.org/
   c) The Turtle Conservation Fund
      http://www.turtleconservationfund.org/
   d) Turtle Conservation Project
      http://www.turtleconservationproject.org/
2. Create a book, poster, or other project to show what you have learned. a) Why are chelonians endangered? b) What is being done to protect them? c) What can kids do to help?
3. Share what you learned with a friend, classmate, or family member. Maybe you can rally some friends to spread awareness for turtle conservation. Look on the Internet to see if there are any turtle watch programs in your area that you and an adult can join. Citizen science programs like these allow everyday people to help scientists observe and protect wildlife.

Books

Beletsky, Les. *Bird Songs*. New York: Chronicle Books, 2006.

Conant, Roger. *Peterson Field Guide: Reptiles and Amphibians of Eastern and Central North America*. New York: Houghton Mifflin Harcourt, 1998.

Dunn, Jon L., and Jonathan Alderfer. *National Geographic Field Guide to the Birds of North America,* Fifth Edition. Washington, D.C.: National Geographic, 2006.

Harrison, Hal H. *Peterson Field Guide: Eastern Birds' Nests*. New York: Houghton Mifflin Harcourt, 1998.

————. *Peterson Field Guide: Western Birds' Nests*. New York: Houghton Mifflin Harcourt, 2001.

McCarthy, Colin. *Eyewitness Reptile*. New York: DK Children, 2000.

Priddy, Roger. *Smart Kids Reptiles*. New York: Priddy Books, 2007.

Projects for the Birder's Garden: Over 100 Easy Things That You Can Make to Turn Your Yard and Garden into a Bird-Friendly Haven. New York: Rodale Books, 2004.

Roth, Sally. *Attracting Birds to Your Backyard: 536 Ways to Create a Haven for Your Favorite Birds*. New York: Rodale Books, 2003.

Stebbins, Robert C. *Peterson Field Guide: A Field Guide to Western Reptiles and Amphibians*. New York: Houghton Mifflin Harcourt, 2003.

Wilson, Hannah. *Life-Size Reptiles*. New York: Sterling, 2007.

Winner, Cherie. *Everything Reptile: What Kids Really Want to Know About Reptiles*. New York: Northword, 2004.

Works Consulted

Alderfer, Jonathan, and Jon L. Dunn. *National Geographic Birding Essentials*. Washington, D.C.: National Geographic, 2007.

Birds Around Us. San Francisco: Ortho Books, 1986.

Casselman, Anne. "Chameleons Evolved Color Changing to Communicate." *National Geographic News,* January 28, 2008. http://news.nationalgeographic.com/news/2008/01/080128-chameleon-color.html

Goldsmith, Timothy H. "What Birds See." *Scientific American,* July 2006: 68–75.

Halliday, Tim, and Mark O'Shea. *Reptiles and Amphibians*. New York: DK Adult, 2001.

Hutchinson, John, PhD. "Dinobuzz: Dinosaur-Bird Relationships." UCMP—University of California Museum of Paleontology, May 9, 2009. http://www.ucmp.berkeley.edu/diapsids/avians.html.

"The Life of Birds | Evolution." *PBS*. April 6, 2009. http://www.pbs.org/lifeofbirds/evolution/index.html.

Ortho's All About Attracting Birds. San Ramon: Ortho, 2001.

Vitt, Laurie J. *Herpetology*. Burlington, MA: Elsevier, 2008.

On the Internet

Audubon: "Citizen Science"
http://www.audubon.org/bird/citizen/

The Birder's Report: "Bird Egg and Nest Identification"
http://www.thebirdersreport.com/egg-and-nest-identification

Bird Watching for Kids:"Science Learning in Bird Watching"
http://biglearning.com/treasurebirds.htm

Cornell University School of Ornithology: "Citizen Science"
http://www.birds.cornell.edu/NetCommunity/Page.aspx?pid=708

Cornell University School of Ornithology's NestWatch: "How to Identify Birds
Nests"
http://www.nestwatch.org/NetCommunity/Page.aspx?pid=595&srcid=265

The Crocodile Is Very Fast
http://www.youtube.com/watch?v=a2j3-wn0TaM&feature=related

The Great Backyard Bird Count: "The Great Backyard Bird Count Is for Kids!"
http://www.birdsource.org/gbbc/kids

National Science Foundation: "The Secret of a Snake's Slither"
http://nsf.gov/news/news_summ.jsp?cntn_id=114941&org=
DMS&from=news

Sialis: "Learn to Recognize Birds, Nests and Eggs that May Show up in Bluebird
Nestboxes"
http://www.sialis.org/nests.htm

Smithsonian National Zoological Park: "Birds for Kids"
http://nationalzoo.si.edu/Animals/Birds/ForKids/default.cfm

Smithsonian National Zoological Park: "Reptiles and Amphibians for Kids"
http://nationalzoo.si.edu/Animals/ReptilesAmphibians/
ForKids/default.cfm

South Walton Sea Turtle Watch Foundation: "Sea Turtle Watch"
http://seaturtlewatch.com/

Yahoo! Kids: "What Is a Bird?"
http://kids.yahoo.com/animals/birds/

Yahoo! Kids: "What Is a Reptile?"
http://kids.yahoo.com/animals/reptiles/

albumen (AL-byoo-mun)—The white of an egg.

archaeopteryx (ar-kee-OP-ter-iks)—Extinct toothed bird from the Jurassic period.

barbs (BARBZ)—Parallel filaments that protect the shaft of a feather.

barbules (BAR-byoolz)—The fringed projections on a feather.

blastoderm (BLAS-tuh-durm)—The layer of cells that encloses an egg's yolk.

blind—A hiding place made by hunters or naturalists for use in nature.

calcite (KAL-syt)—The crystal form of calcium carbonate.

calcium carbonate (KAL-see-um KAR-buh-nayt)—A chemical compound commonly found in rock and chalk.

chalaza (kuh-LAY-zuh)—Either of two spiral bands connecting the yoke to the membrane in an egg. Plural is *chalazae* (kuh-LAY-zee).

cones (KOHNZ)—The receptors in the eyes that are sensitive to bright light and allow people and animals to see color.

dissect (dih-SEKT)—To cut open in order to analyze.

diurnal (dy-UR-nul)—Active during the day.

extinct (ek-STINGKT)—No longer living on Earth.

fossil (FAH-sul)—The remains of a plant or animal.

insulation (in-suh-LAY-shun)—Material that prevents heat gain or loss.

locomotion (loh-kuh-MOH-shun)—The ability to move.

metabolism (muh-TAB-uh-lizm)—The chemical reactions that happen within an organism to support life, such as with food digestion.

nocturnal (nok-TUR-nul)—Active at night.

rods—The receptors in the eye that are sensitive to dim light.

shaft—The hollow spine in the center of a feather.

syrinx (SIR-inks)—The vocal organ of a bird. The plural is *syringes* (sir-IN-geez).

thermosensitivity (ther-moh-sen-sih-TIV-ih-tee)—Ability to feel and react to heat.

ABOUT THE AUTHOR

Colleen Kessler is the author of numerous science books for kids, including *Super Smart Science* and *Hands-On Ecology*, both from Prufrock Press. A former teacher of gifted students, Colleen now satisfies her curiosity full-time as a nonfiction writer. She does her researching and writing in her home office overlooking a wooded backyard in Northeastern Ohio. You can often find her blasting off rockets or searching for salamanders with her husband, Brian, and kids, Trevor, Molly, and Logan, or inspiring schoolchildren to study science and nature. For more information, visit her on the web at http://www.colleen-kessler.com.